AS Economics
UNIT 3

Edexcel

Unit 3: Managing the Economy

Quintin Brewer

Philip Allan Updates
Market Place
Deddington
Oxfordshire
OX15 0SE

tel: 01869 338652
fax: 01869 337590
e-mail: sales@philipallan.co.uk
www.philipallan.co.uk

© Philip Allan Updates 2004

ISBN 0 86003 699 5

This guide has been written specifically to support students preparing for the Edexcel AS Economics Unit 3 examination. The content has been neither approved nor endorsed by Edexcel and remains the sole responsibility of the author.

Printed by Information Press, Eynsham, Oxford

Environmental information
The paper on which this title is printed is sourced from managed, sustainable forests.

Contents

Introduction

■ ■ ■

Content Guidance

■ ■ ■

Questions and Answers

Introduction

Aims

This guide has been written to prepare students for Unit 3 of Edexcel's Advanced Subsidiary (AS) GCE examinations in economics. It provides an overview of the knowledge and skills required to achieve a high grade in the examination for Managing the Economy. This unit introduces the key measures of economic performance and the main objectives and instruments of government policy. It may be broken down into four broad areas as outlined below:

(1) **Key indicators of economic performance:** how the rate of inflation, the level of unemployment, the balance of payments and economic growth are measured.

(2) **Aggregate demand and aggregate supply:** influences on aggregate demand, such as consumption, investment, government expenditure, exports and imports; influences on aggregate supply, such as technological advances and the skills of the workforce; the interaction of aggregate demand and supply, and causes of shifts in AD and AS curves.

(3) **Macroeconomic policy objectives:** the causes, costs and effects of unemployment, inflation, balance of payments disequilibriums and economic growth.

(4) **Policy instruments:** the use of demand-side policies (such as fiscal, monetary and exchange rate policies) and supply-side policies (such as education and training, reduction in trade union power and privatisation) to achieve economic objectives.

This unit forms the basis for work to be covered in Unit 6 (The UK in the Global Economy), which is the synoptic unit. Consequently, it is very important to secure a clear grasp of the material in Unit 3: time spent on achieving this will pay rich dividends not only in terms of the AS examination but also in relation to the A2 examination.

How to use this guide

This guide provides a summary of the knowledge and skills required for Unit 3. It also focuses on examination techniques, including typical examination questions and answers, and explains what examiners are looking for. It should be used as a supplement to a taught course in conjunction with textbooks and other materials recommended by your teacher.

This introduction explains the examination format and the skills that will be tested. It provides tips on revision planning and sitting the examination. A revision programme for the 3-week period before the Unit 3 examination is also included.

The Content Guidance section provides an overview of the subject matter, identifying what has to be learnt and explaining key concepts and models. Typical examination mistakes made by students are shown, as well as links that exist between topics. These are favourite areas for the examiner to set questions on.

The final part of the guide provides questions and answers on the economic concepts and topics in Unit 3. There are five data-response questions covering relevant topics, with a selection of student answers, ranging in quality from grade A to grade C. The examiner's comments that accompany these answers give an insight into how marks are awarded and what pitfalls should be avoided.

Examination format

Unit 3 is the most important in the AS examination because it accounts for 40% of the weighting (and for 20% of the A-level). The paper consists of two data-response questions and candidates are required to answer one of these questions. The amount of time allowed is 1 hour.

The paper is marked out of 40 and is worth a maximum of 120 UMS marks. (UMS stands for the uniform mark system, which scales your actual mark to one that by statistical correction makes it equivalent to any other exam.)

The questions are usually divided into seven parts, the last of which is worth 15 marks and offers the opportunity for extended prose writing. Of these 15 marks, 6 are allocated for evaluation.

Assessment objectives

There are four assessment objectives, or sets of skills, in each unit of AS and A-level economics. The skills are **knowledge and understanding, application, analysis** and **evaluation**. Exam papers are devised specifically to integrate them into questions. In each of the AS units, the first two objectives — knowledge and understanding, and application — are given a higher weighting than the objectives of analysis and evaluation. This is illustrated by the table below:

Objective	Assessment objectives	Weighting
1	**Knowledge and understanding:** demonstrate knowledge and understanding of the subject matter.	30%
2	**Application:** apply knowledge and critical understanding to problems and issues arising from both familiar and unfamiliar situations.	30%
3	**Analysis:** analyse economic problems and issues.	20%
4	**Evaluation:** evaluate economic arguments and evidence, making informed judgements.	20%

Knowledge and understanding

This objective means having a clear grasp of the economic concepts and models relevant to the unit. Questions testing knowledge are likely to begin with the following command words: *define, identify, describe, outline* and *distinguish between*. Knowledge and understanding can be demonstrated in the following ways:

- displaying knowledge of major ideas, terms and concepts
- observing and recalling information
- understanding data
- interpreting data
- predicting consequences

To be successful in this objective, it is vital that you gain mastery of your subject matter. Below is a checklist of the concepts and terms with which you should be familiar:

- retail price index (RPI and RPIX) ✔
- consumer price index (CPI) ✔
- rate of inflation ✔
- unemployment ✔
- claimant count and International Labour Organisation (ILO) measures of unemployment
- balance of payments
- deficit/surplus on the current account of the balance of payments
- gross domestic product (GDP)
- production possibility frontier (PPF)
- standard of living
- aggregate demand (AD)
- equilibrium
- consumption
- investment
- productivity
- injections into the circular flow of income
- public expenditure
- withdrawals (leakages) from the circular flow of income
- multiplier
- aggregate supply (AS)
- economic growth
- full employment
- wealth
- interest rates
- exchange rates
- real income
- real output
- income redistribution
- menu costs
- innovation
- demand-side policies
- fiscal policy
- budget (fiscal) deficit
- budget (fiscal) surplus
- monetary policy
- supply-side policies

Application

This skill involves using the information or data provided in a question, and applying economic concepts to real-world situations — for example, in an explanation of changes in the level of retail sales in an economy. Questions testing application are likely to begin with command words such as *apply*, *illustrate* and *classify*.

Analysis

Analytical skills include the ability to organise and develop a coherent argument using economic concepts. For example, you might use aggregate demand and aggregate supply analysis to explain the economic impact of an increase in interest rates, or production possibility frontiers to demonstrate economic growth. Questions demanding analysis often include the following command words: *analyse*, *explain*, *compare* and *classify*.

Evaluation

Evaluative skills may be demonstrated in a variety of ways, such as:

- comparing and discriminating between different economic theories
- assessing the value or relevance of economic theories in explaining real-world issues
- making a judgement on the basis of evidence/analysis
- making recommendations based on reasoned arguments
- commenting on the relative significance of factors that might explain changes in an economic variable
- distinguishing between fact and opinion

Examples include assessing the relative advantages of using supply-side and demand-side policies to reduce the rate of inflation, or examining the impact of economic growth on living standards. Questions demanding evaluation use command words such as *assess*, *comment on*, *critically analyse*, *examine*, *evaluate* and *recommend*.

How to tackle the examination paper

It is essential that you allocate the hour you have in the exam effectively. A strategy for ensuring this is detailed below:

- Spend the first 5 minutes selecting which question to answer. It is crucial that you do this because you will be able to perform better on some questions than others. Particular attention should be paid to the last part since this carries the most marks.
- When you have selected a question, divide the time available in relation to the mark bases. For example, you should only spend just over 2 minutes on a question worth 2 marks and between 4 and 5 minutes on a question worth 4 marks. This will ensure that you will have about 15–20 minutes to answer the last part, which is worth 15 marks.
- Leave a few minutes to read through your responses at the end of the examination. This will enable you to correct any mistakes.

As with Units 1 and 2, Unit 3 is assessed through data-response questions. There are some important skills involved in answering such questions, which need to be practised. Some of the key techniques are listed below:

- Start by reading the actual questions rather than reading all the prose and data. This not only helps in question selection, but also ensures that you read the information in a more focused way.
- Read the data carefully. In particular, check whether they are in nominal (money) terms or in real terms (when inflation has been discounted); look for relationships.
- Use the data. This may sound obvious, but many candidates under-perform because they write generalised answers without any reference to the information provided.
- Apply economic concepts. Again, this is crucial if marks for application and analysis are to be secured.
- Remember to use diagrams where appropriate. It is highly likely that there will be opportunities to use aggregate demand/aggregate supply diagrams in answering some of the questions. Remember to label them accurately.

- Check the command word carefully and evaluate if required to do so.
- Be precise. Explain key concepts accurately and avoid long-winded sentences.
- Remember that the last part of the question is designed to provide the opportunity (and challenge!) of writing extended prose. It is important, therefore, to use paragraphs and to develop your analysis logically.

Planning your revision

Several strategies and activities may be adopted to ensure that you are well prepared for the examination. The following points offer guidance:

- **Ensure that you know all the information required for this unit.** Edexcel has produced not only a specification (syllabus) but also a web guide. The latter is particularly helpful because it includes additional guidance about what you need to learn for the examination. You can find this on the Edexcel website (**www. edexcel.org.uk**).
- **Practise.** After learning a topic or area of the unit, it is important to ensure that you can apply your knowledge. Use the specimen paper and past papers for this purpose. You can find a specimen paper on the Edexcel website. You could even use examination questions from old specifications for practice purposes.
- **Be sure to attend all lessons immediately prior to the examination.** Most teachers plan their courses to ensure that time is left for revision and testing. The opportunity to ask questions is valuable in helping you to clarify your under-standing. You should welcome the chance to practise answering questions in examination conditions because this will help to reduce nerves, which could impair your performance.
- **Ensure that you have a full set of notes.** Refer to the specification to make sure that you have notes on all the main concepts and subject matter. Add to your class notes by using a textbook or newspaper articles.
- **Organise your notes.** Many students take notes and write answers to questions on file paper. These notes frequently become completely disorganised, which makes it very difficult to revise in a coherent manner. Time spent arranging your notes and learning materials in a logical order will make revision much easier.
- **Consider different methods of revision.** People learn in different ways, so it is important to determine which method suits you. Some suggestions are given below:
  — Summarise key points on index cards.
  — Use 'mind maps' — translate written notes into pictures which can then act as an aid to memory.
  — Make presentations on a particular topic to a fellow student, who will then question you on particular points. Some students find it helpful to record themselves outlining the main issues related to a particular topic. The tape can then be replayed at any time.
- **Devise a structured revision programme.** Obviously, this needs to be linked to revision programmes for other subjects. It is important to set achievable revision targets, or the effect can be very demoralising. An example of a 3-week revision programme is shown below.

A 3-week structured revision plan

Hours	Week 1	Week 2	Week 3
1st	Measurement of GDP, RPI, unemployment, balance of payments.	Aggregate demand: its meaning and key components; movements along and shifts of the AD curve.	Conflicts between policy objectives.
2nd	Causes, costs and effects of unemployment.	Components of AD: consumption, investment, public expenditure, exports and imports.	Policy instruments (1): demand-side policies — fiscal and monetary policy.
3rd	Causes, costs and effects of inflation.	Aggregate supply: movements along and shifts of the AS curve.	Policy instruments (2): exchange rate policy.
4th	Causes, costs and effects of balance of payments surpluses and deficits on current account.	The equilibrium level of real income; cause of changes in this level.	Policy instruments (3): supply-side policies.
5th	Causes, costs and effects of economic growth.	Exam practice: structured essay.	Exam practice: data-response question.

This provides a 15-hour revision programme of 5 hours a week. It is based on the assumption that you have worked consistently through the course and have completed the homework set by your teachers. Obviously, if you have not done this, you will need to spend more time on revision. Given that most students are following four or five AS courses, similar revision programmes for these other subjects will result in 20–25 hours' revision in each of the 3 weeks.

Content
Guidance

Economics consists of two broad areas of study: **microeconomics** and **macro-economics**. Microeconomics is the study of individual markets within the economy and is covered in Units 1 and 2 of the Edexcel AS specification. Macroeconomics considers how the economy functions as a whole and is covered in this unit, Managing the Economy.

This section focuses on essential information, including economic concepts and models, that students need to understand to be successful in Unit 3. The information is organised under the following headings:

- Key indicators of economic performance (p. 13)
- Aggregate demand and aggregate supply (p. 18)
- Macroeconomic policy objectives (p. 26)
- Policy instruments (p. 34)

Key indicators of economic performance

Inflation

Inflation is a sustained rise in the general level of prices.

The **retail price index (RPI)** is a way of measuring inflation in the economy. The points below summarise how the retail price index is calculated:

- A representative sample of the population is selected (7,000 households) and asked to maintain a careful record of their expenditure on a month-to-month basis.
- From this survey the spending patterns of the average family can be derived.
- On the basis of this information, decisions can be taken on the range of goods and services to be included in the index.
- Weights are attached to the goods and services included in the index according to their relative importance in household expenditure.

There are a number of problems with the retail price index which make it difficult to secure an accurate estimation of the rate of inflation:

- There is no typical family. The RPI is only a valid indicator of the rate of inflation for people who spend their income in exact accordance with the weights allocated to each item.
- Weights are changed each year in line with changes in patterns of consumption.
- New goods must be included in the survey and goods no longer in significant use are removed. The inclusion of new goods, such as DVDs, and the removal of other goods such as cassette players, together with changes in weights, means that the index is not measuring price changes of a set range of goods with fixed weights over a period of time.
- There are problems in securing accurate information on prices.
- The RPI is not adjusted to take account of changes in the quality of goods.
- There are distortions. In particular, the RPI is biased towards the spending of those on lower incomes. It does not take into account spending on private medical insurance or saving for private pensions, for example.

Another measure is the **RPIX**. This is the retail price index but with mortgage payments removed. It has been argued that including mortgage repayments in the retail price index can have distorting effects. The government therefore tends to use the RPIX in setting inflation targets for the Bank of England and as a measurement of the true rate of inflation.

Make sure that you understand the differences between the RPI and the RPIX, as it is a popular exam question. You must also recognise the limitations with both measures.

National consumer prices indices within Europe, such as the RPI, vary considerably in how they are constructed and in the range of goods and services that are covered. In order to have a measure of inflation that can be compared with other countries, the chancellor of the exchequer announced in the 2003 budget that he intended to adopt the **harmonised index of consumer prices (HICP)** as the UK's inflation index. In the UK, this index is called the **consumer price index (CPI)**. This price index is an internationally comparable measure of inflation because it is constructed according to standard guidelines across all EU countries. The CPI is similar to the RPIX in that both provide a measure of the changes in the cost of buying a representative basket of goods and services. However, housing costs (including buildings insurance and council tax) are given less weight in the CPI. This explains why the inflation rate, as measured by the CPI, was lower than the rate of inflation measured by RPIX for much of the last decade. As a result, the chancellor has set the target rate of inflation at 2% (as measured by CPI). It is used by the European Central Bank (ECB) when setting interest rates in order to meet the target inflation rate for eurozone countries.

Unemployment

Unemployment is a macroeconomic problem that represents a waste of scarce resources — labour that is not being used. The **percentage rate of unemployment** is the number unemployed divided by the size of the workforce, multiplied by 100. This figure is adjusted to allow for seasonal factors that cause unemployment to be high or low at certain times of the year. Changes in the definition as well as changes in the measurement of official unemployment affect the percentage rate.

Two measures of unemployment are currently used by the UK government. These are the **claimant count** and the **International Labour Organisation (ILO)** measure.

Claimant count

The claimant count measures all those people who are out of work and who are eligible to claim benefits. It provides a monthly estimate of the level of unemployment. It is quick to produce and can provide detailed local information displaying differences between regions. The figures are available at little cost, as they are based on administrative records. However, the claimant count is susceptible to changes in the rules governing people eligible for benefits. All but one of the 40 changes since 1979 have reduced the official claimant count. For example, people over 60 are not entitled to claim unemployment benefit.

International Labour Organisation (ILO)

This measure of unemployment is drawn from research into employment called the **Labour Force Survey (LFS)**. This is a quarterly survey based on a random sample of 60,000 households from across the UK of which private households account for 99%. Headline results are published monthly for the average of three consecutive months. The unemployed are measured as those without a job, who:
- are available for work
- have looked for work in the past 4 weeks

One advantage of this method is that it uses an internationally standardised definition of unemployment, which makes comparisons between countries easier.

However, the ILO is costly and it takes time to compile and publish. Consequently, it is out of date before publication and is subject to sampling errors. The Labour Force Survey may actually underestimate the number of unemployed, as it does not include:

- part-time workers who are actively seeking full-time work
- those who are out of work and who are not actively seeking work, but who are receiving benefit and would take a job if it were offered to them

Differences between the two measures

These two measures of unemployment differ in a number of ways. The claimant count excludes a number of key groups of unemployed workers, such as:

- females who are actively looking for work because they are not entitled to benefits
- males in their fifties or sixties who may be collecting a pension from their previous employer, but who are looking for employment

On the other hand, the claimant count may include some unemployed who would not be included in the Labour Force survey: for example, people may be claiming benefits while actually working in the informal economy.

The balance of payments

The UK balance of payments is a record of all financial transactions between the UK and other countries over a year. It is split into several components. Economists, politicians and the business community study the balance of payments in order to gain information on the UK's current and future international competitiveness and movements of incomes and assets.

The current account

The current account is where payments for purchase and sale of goods and services are recorded. For the Unit 3 exam, this is the part of the balance of payments upon which most emphasis is placed. The current account is important because it provides an indication of the competitiveness of the UK's goods and services. It is the sum of the following elements:

> the trade in goods balance
> (i.e. *value of goods exported – value of goods imported*)
> + the trade in services balance
> (i.e. *value of services exported – value of services imported*)
> + net income flows
> (i.e. *value of interest, profits and dividends earned from overseas assets – value of interest, profits and dividends paid abroad to foreign holders of UK assets*)
> + net current transfers
> (e.g. *the UK's contribution to the EU's budget*)

If the sum of the above items is negative, there is said to be a **current account deficit**, and if the sum is positive, there is said to be a **current account surplus**.

Capital and financial account

The capital and financial account shows long-term capital flows. This includes: foreign direct investment; short-term capital flows (sometimes called 'hot money'), which move between countries for speculative reasons; investments in equities (shares); and changes in gold and foreign currency reserves.

The balance of this account should mirror that of the current account. For example, a £10 billion deficit on the current account should be matched by a £10 billion surplus on the capital and financial account. Inevitably, there are errors and omissions in both accounts, and these are identified in a balancing item designed to reflect any discrepancies.

Gross domestic product, gross national product and national income

Gross domestic product (GDP), gross national product (GNP) and national income (NI) are broadly similar and refer to the *value of goods and services* produced by a country in a year. GDP can also be viewed as the *total income* of everyone in the economy, or as the *total expenditure* on the economy's output of goods and services.

Methods of measuring GDP

The **expenditure method** involves summing together all the major expenditures in the economy. It is calculated as follows:

consumers' expenditure **(C)**
+ public authorities' current expenditure on goods and services **(G)**
+ gross domestic fixed capital formulation ⎫
+ value of physical increase in stocks ⎬ **(I)**
+ exports **(X)**
− imports **(M)**
= **GDP at market prices**
+ subsidies
− indirect taxes
= **GDP at factor cost**
+ net property income from abroad
= **GNP**
− depreciation
= **national income**

This method is particularly useful because the key elements of aggregate demand are identified: C + I + G + X − M (see pp. 18–23).

The **income method** involves adding together all forms of income in the economy, such as wages, profits, rent and interest. The **output method** entails valuing the economy's output of goods and services for one year. Obviously, there are problems in measuring the output of the economy. For example, in the case of government spending, money is spent on public services, such as defence, which are not sold in the market. There are also non-marketed goods and services which are produced but either are not traded or are exchanged without money changing hands, such as DIY.

Each of these methods should give the same result because they are simply different measures of the same process of exchange.

Uses of GDP statistics

GDP, GNP and NI statistics are used for a variety of purposes:

- to compare standards of living between countries and over time
- to build models of the economy so that predictions can be made
- to forecast changes in the economy
- to determine contributions to organisations such as the International Monetary Fund

Nominal and real GDP

Economists call the value of goods and services measured at current prices **nominal (money) GDP**, but this is not very useful in making comparisons of, for example, living standards over time. If prices have doubled without there being any change in quantities, GDP will have doubled — yet it would be inaccurate to say that the economy's ability to satisfy demands has doubled.

A better measure, therefore, tallies the economy's output of goods and services and is not influenced by changes in prices. This measure is called **real GDP**. It is the value of goods and services at constant prices.

Limitations of GDP statistics

There are, however, serious limitations to GDP being a measure of living standards and welfare. These concepts are concerned not only with income but also with quality of life, which is not captured in GDP data. Consequently, comparing living standards between countries and over time is difficult for a variety of reasons, some of which are outlined below:

- **Population size and age distribution.** To take account of differences in population size, it is necessary to calculate GDP per head. However, it is very difficult to account for differences in age distribution.
- **Income distribution.** Measuring living standards through examining differences in GDP per head would only be accurate if the distribution of income were the same in every country. In practice, there are significant differences in income distribution between countries. For example, Brazil's income distribution is much more uneven than Japan's. Consequently, even if GDP per head was similar in each country, there would be significant differences in the living standards of the average citizen in each country.
- **Externalities.** External costs, such as pollution and environmental degradation, might vary.
- **Non-market exchanges.** This includes housework and the informal economy.
- **Quality of life.** Housing, hours of work and holidays are examples.
- **Differences in exchange rates.** For example, the exchange rate of a country might not reflect its true purchasing power.

Changes in any of the above mean that comparisons of living standards over time or between countries are likely to be inaccurate if they are based solely on GDP.

Economic growth

Economic growth is usually measured by examining changes in real GDP per head. There is a detailed consideration of economic growth on pp. 29–31.

Examination skills and concepts

- Understanding the distinction between RPI and RPIX.
- Understanding the significance of RPIX for inflation targets.
- Understanding the distinction between the claimant count and ILO methods of calculating unemployment.
- Understanding the distinction between a surplus and a deficit on the current account of the balance of payments.
- Understanding GDP.

Common examination errors

- Making mistakes when calculating the current account of the balance of payments.
- Failing to understand RPIX and the significance of weightings.

Links with other topics

- Balance of payments (Unit 6).
- Unemployment and inflation in an EU and global context (Unit 6).

Aggregate demand and aggregate supply

Aggregate demand (AD)

The aggregate demand curve shows the relationship between the price level and the level of real expenditure in the economy. It is useful to start with an explanation of the **circular flow of income** diagram.

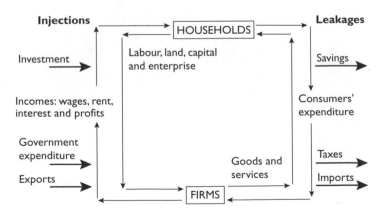

This diagram illustrates the continuous flow of goods, services and payments between businesses and households. The flow of incomes between them will continue at a stable, equilibrium level unless there is a change in injections or leakages.

The circular flow diagram is made up of the following parts:
- **consumers' expenditure (C):** spending by households on goods and services
- **investment (I):** spending by firms on investment goods
- **government expenditure (G):** this includes current spending, for example on wages and salaries
- **exports (X):** spending by foreigners on goods produced domestically
- **imports (M):** spending by firms and households on goods produced abroad

An **injection** is an addition to the circular flow which does not arise from current consumption. Therefore, investment, government expenditure and exports are injections into the circular flow. An increase in any of these will cause national income to rise more than the original increase in expenditure. This is called the **multiplier** effect (see pp. 22–23).

A **leakage** or withdrawal refers to income that is not passed on within the circular flow. Leakages include savings, taxation and imports.

Aggregate demand is the total amount of goods and services that all groups want to purchase at any given level of prices in a particular time period. Therefore, AD is the relationship between the quantity of output demanded and the aggregate price level.

The components of aggregate demand are $AD = C + I + G + (X - M)$.

It is important to note that the aggregate demand curve is different from the micro-demand curve, which shows the relationship between the relative price of a particular product and the quantity of it demanded. The following diagram illustrates an aggregate demand curve that is downward sloping from left to right.

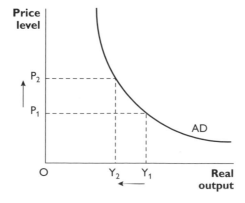

The diagram shows that a rise in the price level from P_1 to P_2 will cause a fall in the amount of real output demanded from Y_1 to Y_2.

Reasons why the aggregate demand (AD) curve is downward sloping

The inverse relationship between the overall price level and the quantity of real output demanded is explained as follows:

- As the general price level rises, the purchasing power of consumers' cash assets is reduced. There is therefore a fall in planned purchases of goods and services, which reduces the quantity of real output demanded. In contrast, if the price level falls, the purchasing power of cash assets increases, leading to an increase in the demand for real output.
- A rise in the price level (relative to other countries) will reduce the international competitiveness of UK goods, so causing a fall in planned demand for exports and a rise in planned demand for imports. There is then a contraction in aggregate demand.
- A rise in the price level will increase the demand for money because consumers will need to hold more money to purchase the higher-priced goods and services. With an unchanged money supply, the rate of interest will rise. With a higher interest rate, the opportunity cost of borrowing money will increase. Firms will therefore put off investment spending, such as on new capital equipment, and consumers may defer plans to purchase goods such as new cars. Once again, there will be a contraction in aggregate demand.

A change in the price level leads to a *movement along the AD curve*. To summarise, movements along the AD curve may be explained by the above three factors. In each case, there was a change in the *price level* with the result that there is a movement *along* the AD curve. As the price level rises there will be less demand for goods and services (i.e. a contraction in aggregate demand). This is shown in the diagram on p. 19. In contrast, as the price level falls there will be more demand for goods and services (i.e. an extension in aggregate demand).

Shifts in the aggregate demand (AD) curve

Changes in non-price factors will cause the *whole aggregate demand curve to shift*. These factors include any of the components of aggregate demand. Therefore, an increase in consumption, investment, government expenditure or exports and imports will cause the aggregate demand curve to shift to the right, whereas a decrease in the above components will cause the aggregate demand curve to shift to the left.

Consumption may rise if there is:

- a fall in unemployment
- a decision by the Bank of England to reduce interest rates, encouraging borrowing for consumer durables
- a reduction in income tax rates
- an increase in asset prices (e.g. share prices or house prices). This is called the **wealth effect**, i.e. when asset prices rise, householders feel wealthier and this encourages them to increase consumption. Of particular significance is mortgage equity release: homeowners take out a mortgage based on the increased value of their property and use this to finance consumption.
- an increase in consumer confidence

Investment may rise if there is:
- a reduction in interest rates
- an expectation of higher profits
- an increase in business confidence

Government spending may increase if there is a change in government policy. For example, the Labour government planned for a significant increase in public expenditure from 2000. Alternatively, the government might decide to increase its expenditure if there is a budget surplus, i.e. when tax revenues are higher than public expenditure.

An increase in exports or a fall in imports might occur if there is:
- a fall in the value of the pound. This would cause a fall in the foreign currency price of UK exports, which would then increase, and a rise in the price of imports into the UK.
- a growth in the world economy, leading to higher demand for UK exports
- an increase in the non-price competitiveness of UK goods (e.g. better quality)

The increase in aggregate demand that would result from any of the above factors is illustrated in the diagram below.

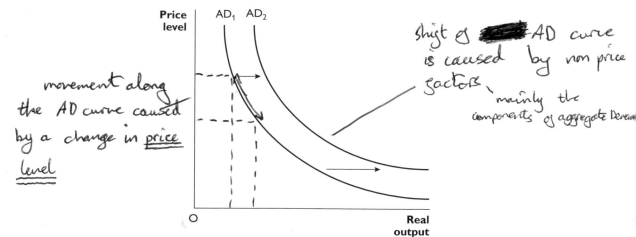

movement along the AD curve caused by a change in price level

shift of the AD curve is caused by non price factors, mainly the components of aggregate Demand

The diagram shows that an increase in aggregate demand will cause a rightward shift in the aggregate demand curve from AD$_1$ to AD$_2$.

A decrease in desired consumption expenditure, investment, government spending or net exports, given a constant price level, leads to a leftward shift in the AD curve.

Consumption may fall if there is:
- a rise in unemployment
- a decision by the Bank of England to increase interest rates, discouraging borrowing for durables and increasing the incentive to save
- an increase in income tax rates

- a decrease in asset prices, e.g. share prices or house prices may fall, causing a negative wealth effect
- a decrease in consumer confidence

Investment may fall if there is:
- an increase in interest rates
- expectations of lower profits
- a decrease in business confidence

Government spending may decrease if there is a change in government policy or if the government decides to decrease its expenditure in order to reduce a budget (fiscal) deficit. Such a deficit is said to exist when government expenditure is greater than the revenues from taxation.

A decrease in exports or a rise in imports might occur if there is:
- a rise in the value of the pound. This would cause an increase in the foreign currency price of UK exports and a decrease in the price of imports into the UK.
- a world recession leading to lower demand for UK exports
- a fall in the non-price competitiveness of UK goods, e.g. poor reliability

The decrease in aggregate demand which would result from any of the above factors is illustrated in the diagram below:

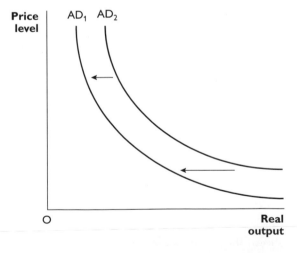

The diagram shows that a decrease in aggregate demand will cause a leftward shift in the aggregate demand curve from AD_1 to AD_2.

The multiplier
The multiplier describes the situation in which an increase (or decrease) in an injection (investment, government expenditure or exports) leads to a more than proportionate increase (or decrease) in GDP. An example will help to demonstrate how the process operates.

If the government decides to increase its expenditure on the National Health Service significantly and to build more hospitals, it not only adds to the total demand for goods and services directly, but also provides extra income for the companies that construct the hospitals and provide the raw materials. These companies will then employ more workers and increase investment in new machinery, thereby generating more income. Although some of this extra income will be taxed or saved, much of it is likely to be spent. The proportion of extra income that is spent on consumer goods is called the **marginal propensity to consume** (MPC): the higher the value of the marginal propensity to consume, the higher the value of the multiplier and the greater its impact on GDP.

The multiplier is calculated as follows:

$$K = \frac{1}{1 - MPC} \text{ where K is the value of the multiplier.}$$

Therefore, if the marginal propensity to consume is 0.75, then the value of the multiplier is:

$$K = \frac{1}{1 - 0.75} = \frac{1}{0.25} = 4$$

Suppose that there is an injection of £20 billion (caused, for example, by increased government expenditure on the NHS). GDP will rise by £80 billion, with a multiplier value of 4.

Aggregate supply (AS)

The aggregate supply curve shows the relationship between the price level and the planned level of output that firms wish to supply. In the short run, the fixed factors of production cannot be increased, but in the long run all factors are variable.

Short-run aggregate supply

The short-run aggregate supply curve is upward sloping, as shown below.

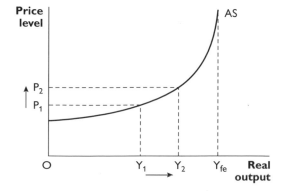

Price changes cause *movements along the AS curve*. Suppliers are usually willing to supply more at higher prices than at lower prices, because the likelihood of making a profit is greater at higher prices. This is because output prices have risen relative to the prices of inputs such as wages and raw material prices. Therefore, a rise in the price level from P_1 to P_2 will cause a planned increase in real output from Y_1 to Y_2.

The AS curve becomes vertical when the full employment level of real output is reached, indicated by Y_{fe} on the horizontal axis. At this point, the economy will be operating on the boundary of its **production possibility frontier** (PPF) (see pp. 29–30). At any output lower than Y_{fe}, the economy will be operating inside its PPF, indicating unemployed resources.

Shifts in the short-run aggregate supply curve

The following diagram shows that an increase in aggregate supply will cause a rightward shift in the short-run AS curve, whereas a decrease in aggregate supply will cause a leftward shift in the short-run AS curve.

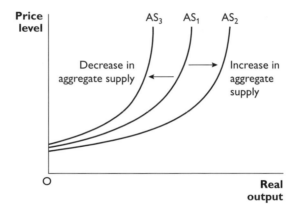

A decrease in AS, and a leftward shift in the short-run aggregate supply curve, may be caused by:

- an increase in money wage rates
- a fall in productivity
- an increase in the price of imported raw materials
- a rise in interest rates
- a decrease in the size of the labour force (e.g. due to emigration)

An increase in AS, and a rightward shift in the aggregate supply curve, would be caused by factors opposite to those listed above:

- a decrease in money wage rates
- a ~~decrease~~ in productivity — *increase in productivity*
- a decrease in the price of imported raw materials
- a decrease in interest rates
- an increase in the size of the labour force (e.g. due to immigration)

Long-run aggregate supply

Long-run aggregate supply is determined by the productive resources available to meet demand and by the **productivity** of factor inputs.

In the short run, producers respond to higher demand by bringing more inputs into the production process and increasing the utilisation of their existing inputs. Supply responds to a change in the price in the short run by moving up or down the supply curve.

In the long-run, all factors are variable and are independent of the price level. The productive potential of an economy is driven by improvements in productivity and an expansion of the available factor inputs. As a result, the long-run aggregate supply curve is vertical.

Shifts in the long-run aggregate supply curve

An increase in the quantity and productivity of factors or an advance in technological factors, such as the development of a new, cheap source of energy, leads to a rightward shift in the vertical long-run aggregate supply.

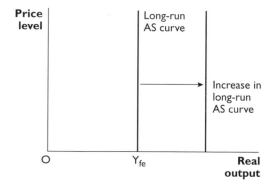

Equilibrium output

Short-run equilibrium is determined by the intersection of the aggregate demand and aggregate supply curves, as shown in the diagram below.

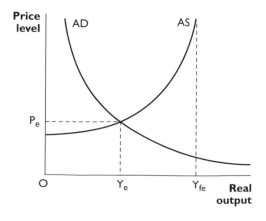

At equilibrium, the price level is P_e and the level of real output is Y_e. Since Y_e is lower than Y_{fe} (the full employment level of GDP), the economy is operating with unemployed resources: in other words, there is an **output gap**. An output gap is defined as the difference between the actual level of GDP and its production possibility frontier.

If the price level is too high, there will be an excess supply of output. If the price level is below equilibrium, there will be excess demand in the short run.

Examination skills and concepts

- Drawing an aggregate demand and aggregate supply diagram to show the equilibrium price level and real output.
- Distinguishing between movements along and shifts of the aggregate demand and aggregate supply curves.
- Identifying factors that might cause a shift in the aggregate demand curve.
- Identifying factors that might cause a shift in the aggregate supply curve.
- Using the basic AD/AS model to analyse the causes of changes in the equilibrium level of real output.

Common examination errors

- Drawing micro demand and supply diagrams instead of aggregate supply and demand diagrams.
- Drawing poorly labelled diagrams.
- Confusion about the factors that cause shifts in aggregate demand and aggregate supply curves.
- Confusion about the direction of movement in aggregate demand and aggregate supply curves.

Links with other topics

- External shocks to the global economy (Unit 6).
- The working of fiscal, monetary and supply-side policies (Unit 6).

Macroeconomic policy objectives

The main objectives of macroeconomic policy are as follows:

- **Full employment.** This literally means that every worker who wants a job at the existing wage rate can have one. In practice, there will always be a degree of unemployment because some workers are temporarily between jobs, a situation known as frictional unemployment. Therefore, full employment is said to exist when a certain percentage of the workforce is unemployed. This is usually between 3% and 5% of the workforce.
- **Price stability.** This takes place when the rate of inflation is zero. In practice, most countries accept that some inflation is desirable, so inflation targets are rarely set at zero.

- **Economic growth.** This takes place when there is an increase in the productive capacity of the country. In practice, growth is usually measured by the annual percentage change in real output of goods and services per capita (GDP per capita).
- **Balance of payments equilibrium.** At its simplest level, this implies that the value of exports is equal to the value of imports. In practice, a disequilibrium in the balance of payments usually relates to the current account and, in particular, to a deficit on this account. Such a deficit implies that the value of goods and services imported is greater than the value of goods and services exported.
- **Concern for the environment.** This objective is, perhaps, best linked to the concept of sustainable development. This refers to development that does not have a detrimental effect on future generations. In recent years countries have given greater priority to the environment, as evidenced by measures such as the banning of CFC gases and attempts to reach worldwide agreements to limit the use of harmful pollutants. However, serious problems have been experienced in reaching agreements and in enforcing them effectively.
- **Income redistribution.** For many decades, governments of all political persuasions have adopted policies designed to redistribute incomes from the rich to the poor with the aim of reducing inequality. In practice, there is still a fairly wide gap between the rich and the poor but some economists think that this is necessary in order to provide the incentives needed for a market economy to operate effectively.

In reality it is difficult for governments to achieve these objectives. The remainder of this section will consider the causes, costs and effects of unemployment, inflation, economic growth, balance of payments disequilibrium, environmental degradation and inequality in the distribution of income. Of these, the first four issues are generally given prominence.

Unemployment

Key types of unemployment

There are three main types of unemployment:

- **Frictional unemployment.** This term is used to describe the normal process of changing jobs. The longer people take when searching for a job, the higher the level of frictional unemployment.
- **Structural unemployment.** This arises when there is a long-term decline in the demand for the products of a particular industry.
- **Cyclical (demand-deficient) unemployment.** This arises when there is a fall in aggregate demand so that the equilibrium level of **real output** is below its full employment level.

Causes of unemployment

The following factors might explain an increase in unemployment in a country:

- **Recession.** This is defined as two quarters of negative economic growth: that is, a period during which real GDP actually falls. A recession is associated with a decrease in aggregate demand.

- **An increase in the value of the country's currency.** This would cause a decrease in the competitiveness of the country's goods, leading to a fall in exports and an increase in imports.
- **An increase in imports from low-wage countries.** There is an increasing trend for multinational companies to relocate their manufacturing plants from developed countries to low-wage countries in the developing world, such as China. Jobs in developed countries are therefore lost.
- **Low productivity.** If productivity is low in relation to other countries, average (unit) costs and prices will be higher. This loss of competitiveness is likely to result in unemployment.
- **External shocks to the economy.** An example of this is an increase in oil prices. Since the demand for oil is inelastic, higher oil prices will usually cause an increase in the rate of inflation. However, higher oil prices usually have a deflationary impact on the world economy because oil-importing countries are faced with a significant increase in leakages, namely, in the value of oil imports. Previous experience suggests that oil exporters are unable to recycle all of their extra revenues, so depressing the world level of aggregate demand. Although the UK has oil supplies, it is likely to suffer from a fall in demand for its exports of manufactured goods as the world economy slides into recession.

Costs of unemployment

Unemployment has several costs:

- **Opportunity cost.** This refers to the output that could have been produced by those workers who are unemployed. Economic growth will be lower than if there was full employment.
- **Costs to the government.** Lower tax revenues from income, expenditure and profits, and increased expenditure on transfer payments contribute to a budget (fiscal) deficit.
- **Costs to firms.** Firms will suffer lower sales, falling profits and loss of economies of scale.
- **Costs to individuals.** People will have lower disposable incomes and lower standards of living.

Benefits of unemployment

Unemployment does provide potential for the economy to expand and can act as a downward pressure on inflation.

Inflation

Causes of inflation

Cost–push

Cost–push inflation is associated with increases in costs of production as a result of changes in the supply side of the economy. It is caused by:

- an increase in costs of production (e.g. an increase in wages not matched by an increase in productivity)

- an increase in raw material prices
- an increase in corporation tax
- a decrease in the value of the pound, causing an increase in the price of imports

Demand–pull

Demand–pull inflation is caused by aggregate demand exceeding aggregate supply. Aggregate demand may rise as a result of an increase in:
- the marginal propensity to consume
- government expenditure, not matched by a rise in taxation
- autonomous investment expenditure
- the value of exports relative to the value of imports

The monetarist view of inflation

According to monetarists, inflation is explained solely in terms of increases in the money supply. At its simplest level, monetarists believe that if the money supply is growing faster than the rate of real growth in the economy, then inflation is inevitable.

Costs of inflation

Inflation has a number of costs:
- **Loss of competitiveness.** Exports of UK goods will fall.
- **Uncertainty.** This could cause firms to reduce investment, which in turn could lead to a fall in the rate of economic growth.
- **Redistribution of income.**
- **Increased industrial wages.** High rates of inflation might result in more strikes as workers try to ensure that their real wages are maintained.
- **Increased government expenditure.** Since many public services are labour intensive, the public sector wage bill is likely to rise sharply.
- **Problems for firms.** Prices will need to be changed more frequently. For example, the prices of goods obtained from coin-operated machines must be updated at regular intervals and cafés and restaurants must change the prices of their menus more often. These costs are called **menu costs**.

Benefits of inflation

Although inflation has serious implications, many economists consider that a low rate of inflation is good for the economy because it:
- reduces the real cost of borrowing, both for firms and households
- encourages investment
- allows workers to gain an increase in their money wages

Economic growth

Economic growth refers to an increase in the productive capacity of an economy — that is, an increase in its ability to produce more goods and services. One method of illustrating economic growth is to use **production possibility frontiers** (PPFs). A production possibility frontier joins together all the combinations of two goods that an economy could produce if all of its resources were fully employed. A diagram illustrating economic growth by means of PPFs is shown below.

Capital goods are manmade resources that are used to produce other goods and services. They include machines, computers and factory buildings. **Consumer goods** give consumers immediate satisfaction, and include food, CDs and clothes.

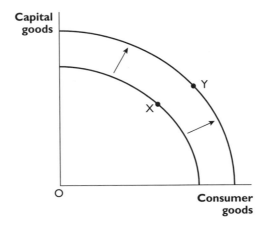

If there is economic growth, the whole PPF will shift outwards. This will enable the economy to move from point X to point Y, and therefore more of both goods will be produced.

Causes of economic growth

The causes of economic growth include:

- **Investment.** This not only increases the productive capacity of a country (leading to a rightward shift of the production possibility frontier), but also generates new income through the multiplier effect.
- **Innovation.** This can be defined as the application of new ideas and new methods of production. To some extent, innovation depends on the amount of research and development that is undertaken in a country. Government expenditure in this area might therefore be significant.
- **A developed financial system.** It is important for businesses to be able to borrow money in order to finance investment. A sound financial system that can channel savings into investment is a significant requirement for economic growth.
- **Availability and discovery of new natural resources.** For example, the difference in the availability of natural resources between the US and Mali is regarded as a major reason why the US has the faster growth rate. New oil supplies in Russia might enable it to achieve a faster rate of growth in the future.
- **Supply-side policies.** These include education, training and privatisation. They are regarded as having particular significance for economic growth and are explained more fully on pp. 34–35.

Different growth rates between countries and between different regions are explained by the extent to which the above factors are available or nurtured.

Benefits of economic growth

The potential benefits of economic growth are felt by consumers, the government, firms and the environment.

For consumers

- It enables consumers to buy more goods and services, and thereby increase their material living standards.
- Workers benefit from longer holidays and shorter working hours.

For the government

- The government receives higher tax revenues from a given tax structure (income taxes and indirect taxes) because incomes are rising.
- Growth makes it easier for the government to redistribute incomes from the rich to the poor.

For firms

- Firms should benefit from higher sales revenue and higher profits.

For the environment

- Richer countries can devote resources to the environment and environmentally friendly methods of production.

Costs of economic growth

Despite its possible benefits, economic growth also brings.the following potential costs:

- **Environmental damage.** This includes increased noise and air pollution, global warming, destruction of the rain forests and water pollution.
- **Depletion of non-renewable resources.** Rapid growth is usually associated with depletion of resources, with the result that coal, oil and gas will eventually run out.
- **Social effects.** During periods of rapid growth, people may be forced out of towns, as they are being developed.
- **Increased stress.** This might result in higher divorce rates, for example.
- **Effects on income distribution.** Growth may be associated with exploitation, as a result of which the owners of the resources benefit disproportionately in comparison to other people in society. The rich may therefore become richer and the poor poorer.

Balance of payments disequilibriums

Balance of payments deficit on the current account

A *deficit* in the current account of the balance of payments implies, broadly, that the value of imported goods and services exceeds the value of exported goods and services.

Causes of a balance of payments deficit on the current account

A balance of payments deficit may be caused by:

- a **high value of the pound** making UK goods uncompetitive
- **cheap imports** from low-wage countries

- a **world recession** causing a slump in demand for UK exports
- a **booming domestic economy** causing imports to be 'sucked' into the UK
- **poor quality, design, reliability** and **availability** of UK goods

Costs of a balance of payments deficit on the current account
A balance of payments deficit may result in:
- **unemployment** (if the cause is a loss of competitiveness of UK goods)
- **loss of confidence** in the UK economy
- a **fall in the value of the pound**, causing imported inflation
- a **fall in gold and foreign currency** reserves

A persistent balance of payments deficit on the current account is likely to lead to a fall in the value of the UK's currency, because the supply of sterling will exceed the demand for sterling on the foreign exchange market. While this might help to increase the competitiveness of the country's goods, it could have inflationary consequences because import prices will increase.

Benefits of a balance of payments deficit on the current account
Despite these problems, a current account deficit might enable consumers to enjoy a higher standard of living than would otherwise be the case. For example, the deficit may be the result of consumers buying very large quantities of imported goods and services.

Balance of payments surplus on the current account
A disequilibrium in the balance of payments might also be said to exist if there is a persistent surplus on the current account.

Causes of a balance of payments surplus on the current account
A surplus on the current account may be caused by:
- a **low value of the pound** making UK goods internationally competitive
- a **world boom** causing an increase in demand for UK exports
- a **recession in the domestic economy** causing lower demand for imports
- **improved quality, design, reliability** and **availability** of UK goods

Costs of a balance of payments surplus on the current account
These include:
- the possibility of **inflationary pressures** because injections (exports) are high in relation to leakages (imports)
- an **increase in the value of the pound** causing an increase in the foreign currency price of exports and a fall in the price of goods imported — this would lead to a fall in the competitiveness of the country's goods and services
- **living standards might fall** if the surplus has been caused by higher exports, resulting in fewer goods being available for domestic consumption

Benefits of a balance of payments surplus on the current account
Despite these problems, a small surplus on the current account is often considered to be desirable because it demonstrates that the country's goods are internationally competitive and enables the country to build up reserves of gold and foreign currency.

content guidance

In turn, this might increase confidence in the economy and help to encourage inward investment.

Environmental degradation

The environment has become a more significant issue and concern in recent decades.

Causes of environmental degradation

Economic growth is often seen as the major cause of damage to the environment. As living standards rise, there is greater pressure to use the countryside to build houses, roads and industrial centres. Higher living standards are also associated with an increased use of energy and all forms of transport which, together with industrialisation, contribute to increased pollution.

Costs of environmental degradation

The results of environmental damage include:

- **more waste** associated with higher growth rates
- **loss of countryside** associated with building houses and new roads
- **global warming** associated with increased car use and energy consumption

Inequality in the distribution of income

Inequality is covered more fully in Unit 5A (Labour Markets), so in the AS course it is not necessary to have a detailed understanding of this issue. It is, however, useful to know some of the possible causes of inequality:

- inherited wealth
- differences in earnings
- ownership of resources, such as shares and houses

Governments recognise that inequality might result in inefficiency. For example, members of a poor 'underclass' may be unproductive and this may affect the economy adversely.

Examination skills and concepts

- Precise understanding of terms, such as balance of payments.

Common examination errors

- Confusing balance of payments and budget (fiscal) deficits and surpluses.
- Failing to appreciate the link between the exchange rate and the competitiveness of a country's goods.

Links with other topics

- The balance of payments (Unit 6).
- Unemployment and inflation in an EU context (Unit 6).
- Production possibility frontiers (Unit 1).
- The causes of economic growth in developing countries (Unit 5B).
- The costs of economic growth (Unit 2).
- Inequality (Unit 5A).

Policy instruments

Supply-side policies

Supply-side economics refers to a broad range of policies aimed at enhancing the performance of the economy by strengthening competitive market forces and increasing economic incentives.

Illustrating supply-side economics

(a) Using production possibility frontiers (PPFs)

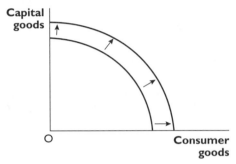

The PPF represents the productive potential of the economy, in this case the combinations of consumer and capital goods which could be employed if all resources are fully employed. Therefore, if supply-side policies are implemented successfully, the productive potential of the economy should increase, so causing an outward shift in the PPF.

(b) Using AD/AS diagrams

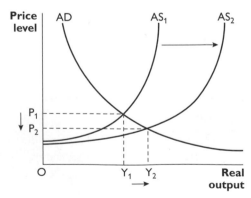

Successful supply-side policies would cause the AS curve to shift to the right, as shown in the diagram above. Consequently, there would be an increase in real output and a fall in the price level.

Supply-side policies in the UK

The rationale of supply-side policies is that the market is more efficient than the government in discovering and transmitting information to ensure the efficient allocation of resources. The ways in which these policies can be applied to the labour market and product market are outlined below.

Supply-side policies in the labour market

The following measures are designed to make the UK labour market more competitive and to reduce real wages:

- **Industrial relations legislation.** For example, in the 1980s the power of trade unions was reduced by legislation that required a ballot of members before unions could take strike action, and made secondary picketing (picketing of firms other than the one where the initial dispute is taking place) illegal.
- **Education and training.** These aim to increase the number of people able to work by developing their skills and making the workforce more flexible. Education and training are recognised by the government as keystones of supply-side policies. One major concern has been the level of attainment in schools.
- **Reductions in income tax.** Supply-side economists believe that lower rates of tax improve incentives for people to work.
- **Reform of the benefits system.** According to supply-side economists, lowering the benefits that the unemployed receive should complement cutting income taxes in giving people an incentive to work.

Supply-side policies in the product market

The following policies are intended to increase competition and efficiency in the UK. If productivity increases, then the amount firms will be able to produce within a given amount of time will increase.

- **Privatisation.** The privatisation of many major industries was introduced in order to increase or to create competition within these industries. Regulators are needed to ensure that competition does actually take place.
- **Deregulation.** Deregulation means opening markets up to greater competition. It invites more competitors in to increase competition and drive prices lower. Examples of deregulation include urban bus transport, electricity supply and parcel delivery services.
- **Free trade.** This aims to encourage competition and keep companies' costs low in order to promote efficiency.

Problems of using supply-side policies

Supply-side polices are effective in the long run, but do not have an immediate impact on macroeconomic policy objectives. For example, policies designed to improve education and training may take many years before they have an impact on the quality and productivity of the workforce.

These policies might also lead to a more unequal distribution of income. For example, cutting unemployment benefits will have an adverse effect on those without jobs, while cutting income tax rates might benefit those on high incomes most of all.

Measures aimed at increasing aggregate supply will be ineffective if the level of aggregate demand is very low.

Demand-side policies

Demand-side policies are designed to influence the level of aggregate demand. They include fiscal policy and monetary policy.

Fiscal policy

Fiscal policy refers to the use of changes in public expenditure (i.e. government expenditure and taxation) to influence the level of real output and the price level.

An example of the impact of fiscal policy: an increase in income tax rates

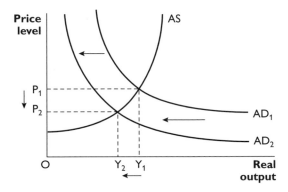

An increase in income tax rates would reduce disposable income. In turn, this is likely to have a direct impact on consumption — with less disposable income, households are likely to cut back on their expenditure, so causing a reduction in aggregate demand. As can be seen from the diagram, this would cause a fall in real income (therefore increasing unemployment) and a fall in the price level. Higher income tax rates could also have a negative effect on incentives, which would cause the aggregate supply curve to shift to the left.

Problems of using fiscal policy

Fiscal policy takes a considerable time to implement. For example, tax changes are usually only announced in the annual budget. There is often a further time lag before they come into effect, although changes in taxes on products such as cigarettes and petrol may be more immediate.

There is often a considerable gap between announcements of changes in public expenditure and their real impact on the economy. For example, a decision to build more hospitals may take years to implement because of the need to secure suitable sites and planning permission.

A further problem is that it is difficult to determine the magnitude of the effect of changes in taxes or public expenditure. Much may depend on the size of the multiplier and on other factors such as consumer and business confidence. For example, attempts to stimulate the economy by cutting taxes and increasing public expenditure may be ineffective if consumer and business confidence is low. This would depress spending by both firms and households.

The use of fiscal policy is hindered by the EU's Growth and Stability Pact, which limits fiscal deficits to 3% of GDP. Although the UK has not yet adopted the euro, the government's desire to join might limit its use of fiscal policy in order to meet this requirement. In order to deal with a large budget deficit the government might be forced to increase taxes and/or reduce public expenditure. Both of these might have undesirable consequences. For example, higher taxes on incomes might act as a disincentive to effort, while cuts in expenditure on education might reduce labour productivity in the future.

Monetary policy

Monetary policy involves the control of monetary variables, such as the rate of interest and the money supply, in order to influence the level of real output and the price level. Since 1997 interest rates have been under the independent control of the Bank of England. It is the Bank of England's Monetary Policy Committee that has the responsibility for meeting the government's inflation target. Using the RPIX measure of inflation, the target was originally set at 2.5% with a 1% margin on either side: in other words, inflation should be maintained within a range of 1.5% to 3.5%. The target set for the Consumer Price Index (from December 2003) is 2%, with a 1% margin either side.

An example of the impact of monetary policy: an increase in interest rates

The rate of interest is the price of money. Interest rates are primarily used by the Bank of England's Monetary Policy Committee to control inflation in accordance with the target set by the chancellor of the exchequer. When setting interest rates, the Bank of England examines a range of data including:

- the output figures, such as GDP
- the current rate of inflation
- the level of unemployment and trends in unemployment
- the rate of increase in average earnings
- the rate of change in retail sales
- the rate of change in house prices and share prices
- the level of consumer debt

The rate of interest affects the economy through its influence on aggregate demand — the higher the rate of interest, the lower the level of aggregate demand. This impacts in several ways:

- **Consumer durables.** Many consumers buy consumer durables on credit. They may therefore decrease their purchases of durables when interest rates are high because repayments will be higher.
- **The housing market.** Houses are often bought with a mortgage, so when interest rates are high, the mortgage repayments will be high and this will deter potential buyers.
- **Saving rates.** Saving is a more attractive alternative when interest rates are high than when they are low, as there is a greater reward for putting money in a bank. This in turn may lead to a reduction in aggregate demand.
- **Exchange rates.** A rise in the UK interest rate is likely to lead to a rise in the value of the pound sterling. A rise in the domestic currency means that import prices

are likely to fall. This would make UK goods less competitive, so UK firms would try to cut prices, thereby causing a downward pressure on the rate of inflation. However, the rise in the value of the pound would also cause the foreign currency price of UK exports abroad to increase. UK firms would, therefore, have an incentive to cut costs and resist wage demands in the UK, in an attempt to make their goods more competitive. This would have the effect of reducing inflationary pressures in the economy.

Examination skills and concepts
- Awareness of the distinction between monetary, fiscal and supply-side policies.
- Understanding of the impact of changes in the value of the pound on the economy.

Common examination errors
- Confusing fiscal and supply-side policies.
- Misunderstanding the effects of changes in the exchange rate.

Links with other topics
- The working of fiscal, monetary and supply-side policies (Unit 6).
- Externalities (Unit 2).

Questions
&
Answers

This section contains five data-response questions that are designed to help your learning, revision and examination preparation.

This section also includes:
- A student answer of grade-A to grade-C standard for each question.
- Examiner's comments about each answer, explaining, where relevant, how the response could be improved. These comments are preceded by the icon *e*.

It should be noted that in most questions you will be required to include aggregate demand and aggregate supply analysis. The inclusion of accurate, carefully labelled diagrams is essential. The answers to the questions and examiner comments on them show that success in the examination depends not only on the ability to demonstrate accurate knowledge and clear understanding, but also on examination technique. In particular, the significance of command words is highlighted.

Question 1

Aggregate demand and aggregate supply

Expenditure on gross domestic product at constant (1995) market prices (€m)

	1996	1998	2000	2002
Personal consumption of goods and services	31,206	35,896	42,678	46,242
Net expenditure by central and local government on current goods and services	8,121	8,999	10,414	12,654
Gross domestic fixed capital formation	10,656	14,697	17,960	18,275
Value of physical increase in stocks	571	1,242	770	8
Exports of goods and services	45,147	64,171	89,166	102,536
Less imports of goods and services	−38,474	−56,356	−76,644	−83,493
GDP at constant market prices	56,891	68,663	84,113	95,499

Source: www.cso.ie/publications/financial/nie.pdf.

(a) Explain what is meant by 'gross domestic product at constant (1995) market prices'. (3 marks)

(b) (i) What are the components of aggregate demand? (2 marks)

(ii) Why does the aggregate demand curve slope downwards? (4 marks)

(c) Using an aggregate demand and aggregate supply diagram, explain the effects of an increase in investment on real output and on the price level. (6 marks)

(d) How is the current account of the balance of payments calculated? (2 marks)

(e) Assess the significance of two factors that might account for changes in the level of consumer expenditure between 1996 and 2000. (8 marks)

(f) To what extent does the increase in gross domestic product at constant (1995) market prices between 1996 and 2002 indicate an increase in living standards? (15 marks)

■ ■ ■

Candidate's answer

(a) This means the amount of goods and services produced during a year after discounting the effects of inflation. **2/3 marks**

e This is an imprecise response because GDP should be defined as the value of goods and services produced. However, the candidate does recognise that the data are given in real terms.

ata-response question 1

(b) (i) The main components of aggregate demand are consumption, investment, government expenditure and exports minus imports, i.e. AD = C + I + G + (X − M).   **2/2 marks**

e This answer would receive full marks. With such a small mark base, it is unnecessary to write more than this.

(ii) The aggregate demand curve is downward sloping because when the price level falls people can afford to buy more goods, since they can buy more with each pound they earn, i.e. their real incomes have risen.

Another reason why the AD curve slopes downwards is that, if there is a fall in the price level in the UK relative to other countries, then UK goods will become more competitive, meaning that exports will rise. This will cause a rise in AD.   **4/4 marks**

e Two valid reasons are offered to explain why the AD curve slopes downwards and, although the explanations could be more concise, the candidate has done enough to earn full marks. The answer would have been enhanced by including a diagram of an AD curve.

(c) Investment is one of the components of aggregate demand and so an increase in investment will cause a rightward movement in the AD curve. In addition, investment also increases AS because there will be more factories and machinery, which means that the country is able to produce more. The diagram below shows the effect of an increase in aggregate demand and aggregate supply.

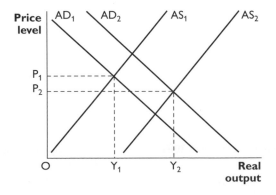

The rise in investment will cause both the AD and AS curves to shift to the right. This will cause the price level to fall from P_1 to P_2 and real output to rise from Y_1 to Y_2.   **6/6 marks**

e This is an effective answer which would receive full marks. The candidate has understood that an increase in investment will affect both AD and AS. All too often candidates ignore the impact on AS. Such answers could only be rewarded with a maximum of 3/6.

(d) The current account of the balance of payments is calculated by finding the difference between taxes and government expenditure. **0/2 marks**

> *e* The candidate's answer is incorrect and reflects a common confusion between budgets and the balance of payments. To determine whether there is a *budget* surplus or deficit, it is necessary to deduct government expenditure from tax revenue. However, the balance of payments is the external balance: it relates to the UK's trade with other countries. The balance of payments on the current account is the sum of the following: the trade in goods balance, the trade in services balance and net investment income.

(e) During the period from 1996 to 2000 consumer spending was rising which might be the result of a fall in interest rates which would make it less attractive to save and cheaper for people to borrow money so that they can buy more goods and services and this would explain why people were spending more money and not putting savings into banks.

Another reason which might explain the rise in consumer spending could be that unemployment was falling, which meant that more people were in jobs and had incomes to spend. **4/8 marks**

> *e* This answer illustrates two problems typical of many examination answers. First, the answer is long-winded and not very coherent. Splitting the first paragraph into shorter sentences would have helped the candidate to marshal his or her ideas more clearly and effectively. Second, the answer ignores the command word 'assess', which means that some evaluation is required — for example, a consideration of the relative importance of the two factors mentioned. Nevertheless, this answer does identify two relevant reasons for the increase in consumers' expenditure and there is some valid reasoning.

(f) The fact that GDP has risen in real terms means that real incomes should have risen in the country. Therefore, people should be better off and able to afford more goods and services. With higher incomes, people can afford to go on more exotic holidays and buy more luxury goods. If people are earning more money, the government will be receiving more tax revenue, too, which can be used to improve public services, such as health, education and transport.

However, not all people will have benefited from the increase in GDP. People who have lost their jobs would be worse off, as would women who have stopped work to have children. Income distribution might have become less equal: while some may be better off, the majority of people may not have experienced an increase in income. It is necessary to take account of changes in population; to judge whether living standards have increased, it is necessary to measure changes in real GDP per head.

An important issue is that GDP is not an accurate measure of living standards because a person's standard of living depends not only on his or her income but

ata-response question 1

also on quality of life. Therefore, it is necessary to consider other factors such as levels of pollution and congestion; the quality of housing; the amount of holidays and hours of work. British workers are said to have the longest working hours in the EU. They also spend the most time commuting to work. Both of these factors reduce living standards.

Usually, therefore, an increase in real GDP per head would imply an increase in living standards, but other things must be considered. This makes it difficult to be sure that the rise in GDP between 1996 and 2002 has resulted in a rise in living standards.   **13/15 marks**

e This is a good answer because the candidate has considered both sides of the question. Of particular importance is the candidate's recognition that GDP and living standards are different concepts, so that a rise in GDP does not automatically mean that there is a rise in living standards. There is also a brief conclusion that attempts to answer the question directly. Further development of this last paragraph might have ensured full marks.

Scored 31/40 = grade A

Question 2

Consumer spending

For the last 7 years, household consumption has risen at an annual rate averaging 4%, far faster than GDP. It has been sustained throughout by rising real incomes and falling unemployment and, more recently, by the strength of the housing market.

Prompt and pre-emptive easing of monetary policy helped Britain to avoid the recession that engulfed the other G7 economies. It also underpinned the housing market. 5 At its height in the autumn of 2002, house price inflation was running at 30%. This also encouraged mortgage equity withdrawal: that is, homeowners borrowing money based on the increased value of their houses.

In terms of the outlook for consumer spending, 2003 was supposed to be different. For a start, higher taxes in the form of the April rise in national insurance contribu- 10 tions were expected to hold back private consumption. Government expenditure was expected to take up the running, and the combination of global recovery and the fall in the value of sterling opened up the possibility of more balanced growth.

The squeeze on household budgets is real. Household earnings growth is running at a modest 3–3.5%. This means that — measured net of the tax and price index (which 15 captures the rise in national insurance contributions) — the growth in real earnings has turned negative. There is, however, a huge gap between falling real earnings and the 6% rise in retail sales volumes in the year to June 2003.

Source: adapted from the *Sunday Times*, 3 August 2003.

(a) **Explain what is meant by:**
   (i) **GDP** (2 marks)
   (ii) **'rising real incomes' (line 2)** (2 marks)
(b) **Using an aggregate demand and supply diagram, explain how the 'prompt and pre-emptive easing of monetary policy helped Britain to avoid the recession that engulfed the other G7 economies' (lines 4–5).** (6 marks)
(c) **Explain what is meant by injections and leakages and give an example of each from the passage.** (4 marks)
(d) **How might the 'huge gap between falling real earnings and the 6% rise in retail sales volumes' (lines 17–18) be explained?** (5 marks)
(e) **Assess the significance of the housing market in explaining the strength of consumer expenditure.** (6 marks)
(f) **Evaluate the likely impact on the UK economy of national insurance tax rises and a simultaneous increase in government expenditure.** (15 marks)

■ ■ ■

data-response question 2

Candidate's answer

(a) (i) GDP means gross domestic product.   **0/2 marks**

> *e* At this level, candidates are expected to know what the letters GDP stand for. What is required here is a definition that makes clear that GDP represents the value of goods and services produced by a country in a year.

(ii) This means that incomes are rising after adjusting for price changes. Consequently, people can afford to buy a larger quantity of goods and services.
                                                                                2/2 marks

> *e* This is a succinct and accurate answer that deserves full marks.

(b) The easing of monetary policy implies that the Bank of England reduced interest rates. A fall in interest rates will cause a rise in the marginal propensity to consume and a fall in the marginal propensity to save because the opportunity cost of saving will have risen. Similarly, there will be a greater incentive to borrow because the interest rate on loans will have fallen. Therefore, both households and firms may take out more loans, leading to a rise in both consumption and investment. This increase in these components of aggregate demand will cause the AD curve to shift to the right as shown in the diagram below. This will cause a rise in real output from Y_1 to Y_2, so helping the UK to avoid a recession.

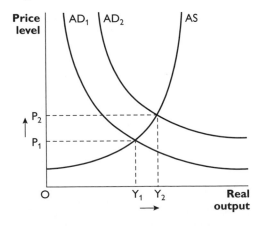

                                                                                6/6 marks

> *e* This very sound answer shows understanding of the phrase 'an easing of monetary policy'. It is supported by an accurate diagram and would earn full marks.

(c) Injections are additions to spending in the circular flow of income. They refer to any spending that does not arise out of consumer spending. An injection mentioned in the passage is government expenditure.

Leakages are withdrawals of potential spending from the circular flow. Savings are a leakage because income that could have been spent is held back by consumers.   **3/4 marks** *e* This answer is correct, but it would not be awarded full marks because the example of leakages is not taken from the passage. This illustrates the importance of reading the question carefully and making appropriate use of the information provided.

(d) The fact that retail sales are rising while real earnings are falling is unusual. It could be explained by consumers using their savings in order to fund higher spending. Running down savings is a way people can increase spending even if their incomes are not rising.

The passage suggests that consumers are taking out loans on the basis of the increased value of their houses. This means that they are able to buy more goods and services.

Another possibility is that consumers are using their credit cards more and running up larger debts. **5/5 marks**

e This is a very good answer that considers three different reasons to explain the paradox. In fact, it would have been sufficient to refer to just two factors, emphasising the one mentioned in the passage — equity release.

(e) The housing market is important in the UK because home ownership is very large — about 70% of households are owner-occupiers.

Changes in house prices, therefore, have an impact on consumer spending. However, other factors might also explain the strength of consumer spending, such as the falling rate of unemployment and low interest rates. **3/6 marks**

e This answer does not explain fully the significance of the housing market for the level of consumer expenditure. There is no consideration of the significance of rising house prices for consumer confidence, nor is there any mention of the 'wealth effect'. However, the evaluation points in the last sentence are valid.

(f) The increases in national insurance will decrease disposable income — that is, income after tax. If disposable incomes are lower, then consumers are likely to spend less, so causing a fall in consumers' expenditure unless workers do more overtime or take on second jobs in order to maintain their incomes. Alternatively, consumers could run down their savings as a means of maintaining their spending.

An increase in government expenditure will cause national income to rise through the multiplier effect. For example, if the government spends money on building new hospitals, then new jobs will be created providing incomes for workers who were previously unemployed. If these incomes are spent, then other firms (and workers) will benefit. Government expenditure is a component of aggregate demand and so if it increases, AD will rise.

The overall effect of higher national insurance taxes and higher government expenditure depends on a number of factors. One of the most important is the amount by which national insurance contributions are increased and the amount by which

government expenditure rises. There may also be a difference in the timing of the effects — the national insurance contributions might have a more immediate impact than the rise in government expenditure, especially if government spending is on long-term capital projects. **12/15 marks**

e The implications of higher national insurance contributions and higher government expenditure are outlined well, but the answer could have been improved by the inclusion of an AD/AS diagram. The candidate makes two effective evaluation points.

Scored 31/40 marks = grade A

Question 3

The UK economy

UK macroeconomic performance indicators, 2001–03

	2001	2002	2003
GDP (%)	2.1	1.8	1.9
Services (%)	3.4	2.7	2.2
Manufacturing (%)	−2.4	−4.0	0.1
Construction (%)	3.6	7.5	5.0
ILO measure of unemployment (millions)	1.43	1.52	1.53
RPI (%)	1.8	1.7	3.0
RPIX (%)	2.1	2.2	2.9
Trade in goods balance (£bn)	−33.5	−35.2	−38.0
Current account balance (£bn)	−12.5	−8.7	−20.0

Note: data for 2003 are estimated; percentage figures show annual percentage changes in real terms.

Source: *HSBC Economic Review*, July 2003, issue 29.

(a) Contrast the performance of the manufacturing and service sectors of the economy in 2001 and 2002. (3 marks)

(b) Outline one advantage of using the **ILO** measure of unemployment instead of the claimant count measure. (3 marks)

(c) (i) What is the main difference between the **RPI** and **RPIX** measures of inflation? (2 marks)

(ii) Explain two possible implications of the trend in the rate of inflation. (6 marks)

(d) Examine two likely economic effects of the changes in manufacturing output in 2001 and 2002. (8 marks)

(e) How is it possible for the current account balance to be smaller than the trade in goods balance during 2001–03? (3 marks)

(f) Assess the effects on the economic variables in the table if the **Monetary Policy Committee** increased interest rates at the beginning of 2004. (15 marks)

■ ■ ■

data-response question 3

Candidate's answer

(a) Manufacturing output fell in both 2001 and 2002 but the fall in output was greater in 2002 than in 2001. In contrast, the output of the service sector increased in both years, although it rose less quickly in 2002 than in 2001.   **3/3 marks**

e This is a precise answer that shows a clear understanding of the data.

(b) The ILO measure of unemployment involves a survey of the workforce to determine who has been looking for work in the last 4 weeks and who is available for work. This gives a more accurate measure of the true level of unemployment than the claimant count, which only measures those who are out of work and are eligible to claim the Job Seeker's Allowance.   **3/3 marks**

e This is a sound answer. Another relevant point would be that the ILO measure is more useful when making international comparisons of unemployment.

(c) (i) The RPIX measure of inflation excludes changes in mortgage interest rates whereas the RPI includes this item.   **2/2 marks**

e This is enough to gain full marks because the key point has been identified.

(ii) The rate of inflation is increasing. This could mean that UK goods might become less competitive if the UK's rate of inflation is higher than that of other countries. In turn, this could cause a deficit in the trade in goods balance.   **3/6 marks**

e There is really only one point made in this answer. In order to secure the other 3 marks it would be necessary to consider another implication. For example, the rise in the rate of inflation might lead the Bank of England to raise interest rates. This could result in a slowdown in consumer spending and a higher rate of unemployment.

(d) With the decline in manufacturing output, it is likely that unemployment will increase. This might also lead to a fall in aggregate demand since incomes will fall. However, the impact on unemployment might not be significant if the workers made redundant are able to find jobs in the expanding service sector.   **4/8 marks**

e As far as it goes, this is a sound answer, but the candidate has considered only one economic effect rather than the two demanded by the question. A second point might argue that the decline in the manufacturing industries could have been caused by the high value of the pound, making UK exports more expensive and imports cheaper. This could lead to a deterioration in the trade in goods balance (the value of goods exported minus the value of goods imported).

(e) The current account balance includes the trade in services balance and net investment income as well as the trade in goods balance. A surplus on the trade in services balance would explain why the current account balance is smaller than the trade in goods balance.   **2/2 marks**

e This answer shows a clear understanding of the current account of the balance of payments and provides a convincing response to the question.

(f) An increase in interest rates is likely to cause a decrease in aggregate demand, because consumers are likely to save more and spend less. This is because higher interest rates make borrowing more expensive and saving more attractive, so causing consumption to fall. This is likely to cause a fall in GDP, which means that unemployment is likely to increase.

Lower aggregate demand should bring about a fall in the rate of inflation, so RPI and RPIX should go down.

With lower consumer spending there will be a reduction in the amount of goods imported, so this should mean a fall in the deficit on the trade in goods balance.

6/15 marks

e This is a reasonable summary of some of the likely effects of higher interest rates. It could have been improved if a diagram had been included and if the points had been developed more fully. Moreover, there is no evaluation, so the 6 marks allocated for evaluation are lost. The candidate could have considered the following evaluative points:
- Higher interest rates might have little impact if there is strong world growth, leading to higher exports.
- Consumer spending might continue to rise if the housing market remains strong.
- Rising government expenditure might offset the effect of higher interest rates.

Scored 23/40 = grade B

Question 4

Economic growth

Table 1   *Average annual growth rates in selected countries, 1980–2001 (%)*

	1980–90	1990–2001
UK	3.2	2.7
China	10.3	10.0
Ireland	3.2	7.7
France	2.4	1.9
Germany	3.6	1.8

Source: World Development Report, 2002.

Extract 1

Economic growth is one of the main objectives of macroeconomic policy, but it is often view as a mixed blessing. During a period of economic growth, not only are there a range of benefits to consumers but there are significant advantages for firms and for the government. However, growth can be destructive: it leads to a depletion of resources and serious external costs may be associated with it.

(a) Apart from economic growth, identify three other major objectives of macroeconomic policy. (3 marks)

(b) How is economic growth usually measured? (2 marks)

(c) With reference to Table 1:

　(i) Outline two factors that might explain the difference in growth rates between the UK and one other country in the period 1990–2001. (4 marks)

　(ii) Explain the significance for living standards of the change in Germany's growth rate between 1980–90 and 1990–2001. (4 marks)

(d) (i) Using an aggregate demand and aggregate supply diagram, explain the effect of supply-side policies on the price level and the level of real output. (4 marks)

　(ii) Assess the effectiveness of supply-side policies as a means of increasing the rate of economic growth. (8 marks)

(e) To what extent do the costs of economic growth outweigh the benefits? (15 marks)

■ ■ ■

Candidate's answer

(a) The main objectives of macroeconomic policy are full employment, stable prices and a stable balance of payments. **2/3 marks**

> *e* The first two objectives are correct, but no marks would be awarded for the last objective because it is too vague. A stable balance of payments would not be desirable if there was a huge deficit on the current account.

(b) Economic growth is measured by changes in GDP. **0/2 marks**

> *e* This is an imprecise answer because it ignores the fact that GDP might rise as a result of inflation. Growth is usually measured by changes in real GDP, but it should be noted that this measure might not be accurate because actual GDP could be above or below the productive potential of the economy.

(c) (i) One factor that might explain why the UK's growth rate is lower than Ireland's is that Ireland has been very successful in attracting investment by foreign firms. Investment not only increases GDP through the multiplier process, but also increases the productive capacity of the country. Ireland might have achieved a faster growth rate than the UK because it has been given grants by the EU to develop its infrastructure. **3/4 marks**

> *e* The first point has been explained well and would score 2/2. However, the second point should have been developed in order to show how improvements in infrastructure might lead to a higher growth rate. Additionally, the candidate should have tried to demonstrate why Ireland's infrastructure is superior to the UK's.

(ii) Between 1980–90 and 1990–2001 Germany's growth rate fell from 3.6 to 1.8%. This means that living standards would be falling because people would be getting lower incomes. **0/4 marks**

> *e* This is a common error. The correct interpretation of these figures is that GDP and therefore living standards were still rising in the period 1990–2001 but *at a slower rate* than during 1980–90.

(d) (i)

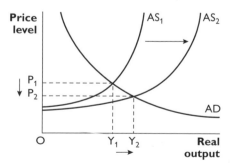

Supply-side policies cause the aggregate supply curve to shift to the right. This will cause an increase in real output from Y_1 to Y_2 (and an increase in employment) and a fall in the price level from P_1 to P_2. **4/4 marks**

data-response question 4

e The diagram is not only clear but has been labelled correctly and the supporting explanation is concise. The answer would be awarded full marks.

(ii) As shown above, supply-side policies are aimed at increasing aggregate supply by increasing incentives and competition. One policy is to improve education and training. This would help to increase the productivity of the workforce. However, these policies take a long time to work, so the results might not be felt for several decades. Another policy that might be used is privatisation. This transfers ownership of industries from the public sector to the private sector. These firms would have greater incentive to be efficient because of the profit motive and increased competition. However, privatisation might simply result in private monopolies that could exploit consumers.

The government could reduce unemployment benefits, so giving the unemployed more incentive to find jobs. If these workers find jobs, then output should increase. However, this policy would not work if aggregate demand is very low and few jobs are available. It would also lead to a less even distribution of income.   **8/8 marks**

e This is a sound answer that covers several valid policies. There is also some effective evaluation of each of the points made.

(e) There are several costs of economic growth. First, there are external costs such as pollution and the loss of countryside as more roads are built. Growth leads to the depletion of resources because more raw materials are needed to produce the extra goods being demanded. There is also an opportunity cost of growth; in order to shift the PPF outwards it is necessary for the country to produce more capital goods. However, to do this fewer consumer goods can be produced in the short run, so reducing current living standards.

There are numerous benefits of growth. First, consumers will have higher incomes which enable them to buy more consumer goods. It is also likely that consumers might benefit from longer holidays and shorter working hours. The government should benefit from higher tax revenues which could be used to improve the health service. Firms would gain higher profits as a result of increased sales.

9/15 marks

e This is a good outline of the costs and benefits of economic growth, but the candidate never really addresses the question. The 6 evaluation marks would be lost because no conclusion or judgement is made as to whether the costs of growth are greater than the benefits. Credit, however, would have been given for making comments such as the fact that economic growth would enable the government to spend more money on cleaning up the environment, thereby reducing the costs of growth.

Scored 26/40 = grade B

Question 5

Interest rates

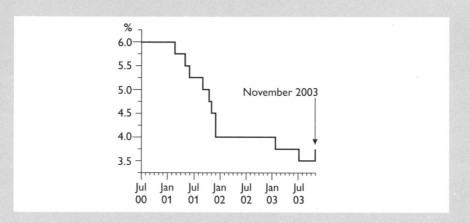

The Bank of England's base interest rate

Source: Bank of England, minutes of Monetary Policy Committee, November 2003.

In November 2003, the Bank of England's Monetary Policy Committee (MPC) decided to increase interest rates from 3.5% to 3.75%, the first increase for 3 years. In arriving at this decision the MPC considered a variety of factors, some of which were conflicting. A selection of these are listed below:

- Personal debt had grown more than 50% since 1997, twice as fast as incomes, and stood at £5,330 per person.
- Mortgage debt was £890 billion or almost £25,000 per household.
- House prices were rising by an average of over 10%.
- Manufacturing output had fallen by 0.2% in the third quarter of 2003.
- Business investment had been declining.
- Earnings were growing at an annual rate of 3.7%, up 0.2% on the previous month.
- Retail sales grew 3.5% faster than in the same month in 2002.
- There was a record trade deficit of £3.9 billion in September 2003 and the deficit was growing larger.
- The RPIX measure of inflation was relatively stable at 2.7%.

(a) **From the information provided, estimate the amount by which annual real earnings were rising.** (2 marks)
(b) **Outline two factors that might explain the increase in personal debt since 1997.** (4 marks)
(c) **Analyse the likely impact of an increase in interest rates on the level of aggregate demand.** (6 marks)

ata-response question 5

(d) (i) **Does the growing trade deficit represent an injection or a leakage?** (2 marks)

   (ii) **Explain why the deficit on the current account balance of the balance of payments might be lower than the trade deficit.** (3 marks)

(e) **With reference to the concept of the multiplier, examine the likely effects of 'declining business investment'.** (8 marks)

(f) **Given the information provided, do you think that the MPC should have increased interest rates? Justify your answer.** (15 marks)

■ ■ ■

Candidate's answer

(a) Real wages have risen by 3.7%. **0/2 marks**

> *e* This in incorrect. To calculate real earnings it is necessary to deduct the rate of inflation from the increase in nominal earnings. Therefore, the calculation would be 3.7% − 2.7% = 1%.

(b) People have been more willing to take on personal debt because interest rates have fallen. In addition, unemployment has been going down. **2/4 marks**

> *e* Although two relevant points have been identified, there is no explanation of their significance. Consequently, only 2 marks would be awarded. The points could have been developed as follows: lower interest rates make borrowing cheaper and saving less attractive; therefore people are more willing to take on debts. The reduction in the unemployment rate might lead to increased consumer confidence, which in turn might lead to increased borrowing.

(c) Higher interest rates are likely to lead to a lower level of business investment because borrowing has become more expensive. Similarly, consumers are likely to reduce their expenditure because there is an increased incentive to save, while interest rates on loans are higher, discouraging borrowing. Since two of the components of aggregate demand have decreased (consumption and investment), there will be a fall in aggregate demand. **4/6 marks**

> *e* This is a good answer, but the impact on consumer spending could have been developed further by a reference to mortgage interest rates, i.e. higher interest rates will cause mortgage interest to increase, leaving households with less money available for spending on other consumer goods and services.

(d) (i) A trade deficit represents an injection into the circular flow of income because it results from higher consumer spending. **0/2 marks**

> *e* This answer is incorrect because a growing trade deficit implies that imports (a leakage) are rising at a faster rate than exports (an injection). Imports are a leakage because money spent on foreign goods forms part of the national income of other countries.

(ii) The balance of payments on the current account includes not only the trade in goods balance but also the trade in services balance, which is usually in surplus. Therefore, the current account deficit is likely to be lower than the trade in goods deficit. **2/3 marks**

e Although this answer is good, it is incomplete because it omits two elements of the balance of payments on the current account, namely net investment income (interest, profits and dividends) and transfers, e.g. the UK's contribution to the EU budget.

(e) When investment declines there is a fall in aggregate demand, because investment is one of the components of aggregate demand, i.e. $AD = C + I + G + (X - M)$. This will cause a fall in the level of real output and in the price level, as shown in the diagram below.

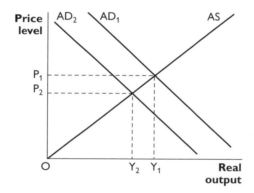

Since real output has fallen, there is likely to be an increase in unemployment. The overall effect on the price level and on real output depends on how much investment falls. **4/8 marks**

e The candidate's answer is good as far as it goes, but no mention is made of the multiplier, which was a specific requirement of the question. There could also have been a reference to the impact of declining investment on aggregate supply. The final sentence includes some evaluation, but this could have been developed more fully.

(f) There is much evidence to support the increase in interest rates. For example, the Bank of England would have been concerned about the rise in household debt and mortgage lending. The low interest rates are encouraging a boom in the housing market, which cannot go on for ever. Higher interest rates are needed to prevent the housing boom from getting out of control with an inevitable crash sometime in the future. The rising trade deficit is another cause for concern. Higher interest rates would help to curb consumer spending and so limit spending on imports. **7/15 marks**

ata-response question 5

e Although some valid points are made, this is a brief response to the question with the largest mark base. Several other points could have been mentioned. For example, the rate of inflation is currently above its target rate and, with earnings rising faster than prices, demand–pull inflation might occur. This factor might have encouraged the Monetary Policy Committee to increase the rate of interest. Another weakness is that there is no reference to factors which might suggest that an increase in interest rates is unwise. For example, business investment and manufacturing output are falling. A rise in interest rates might make the situation worse for the manufacturing sector, especially if the exchange rate was to rise following an increase in the interest rate. Reference could also have been made to factors not included in the information provided, such as the state of the labour market (unemployment trends) or the state of the world economy.

Scored 19/40 = grade C